THE
ANGEL
OF THE SEA
Bed and Breakfast

COOKBOOK

CAPE MAY, NEW JERSEY

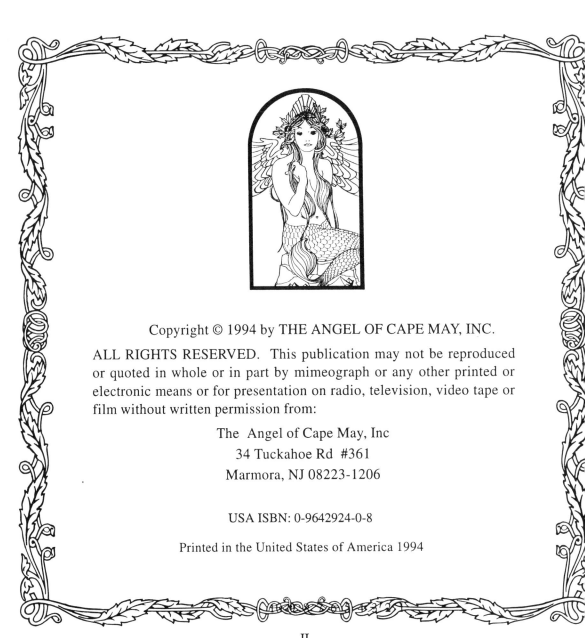

The Angel of Cape May, Inc
34 Tuckahoe Rd #361
Marmora, NJ 08223-1206

USA ISBN: 0-9642924-0-8

Printed in the United States of America 1994

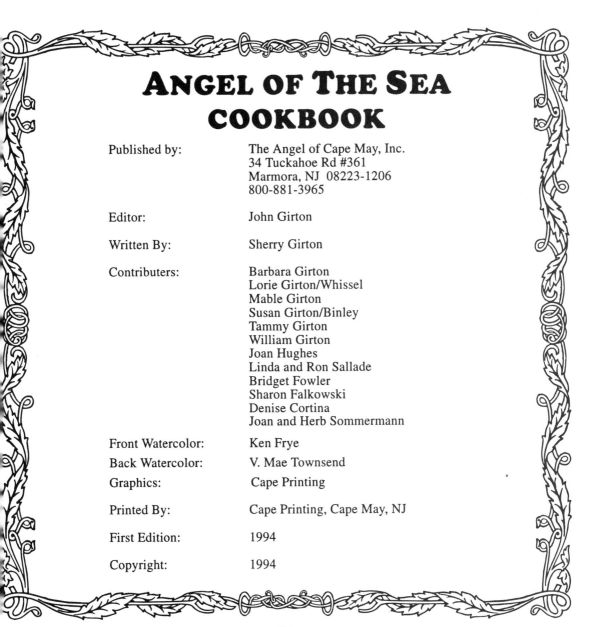

ANGEL OF THE SEA
COOKBOOK

Published by:	The Angel of Cape May, Inc. 34 Tuckahoe Rd #361 Marmora, NJ 08223-1206 800-881-3965
Editor:	John Girton
Written By:	Sherry Girton
Contributers:	Barbara Girton Lorie Girton/Whissel Mable Girton Susan Girton/Binley Tammy Girton William Girton Joan Hughes Linda and Ron Sallade Bridget Fowler Sharon Falkowski Denise Cortina Joan and Herb Sommermann
Front Watercolor:	Ken Frye
Back Watercolor:	V. Mae Townsend
Graphics:	Cape Printing
Printed By:	Cape Printing, Cape May, NJ
First Edition:	1994
Copyright:	1994

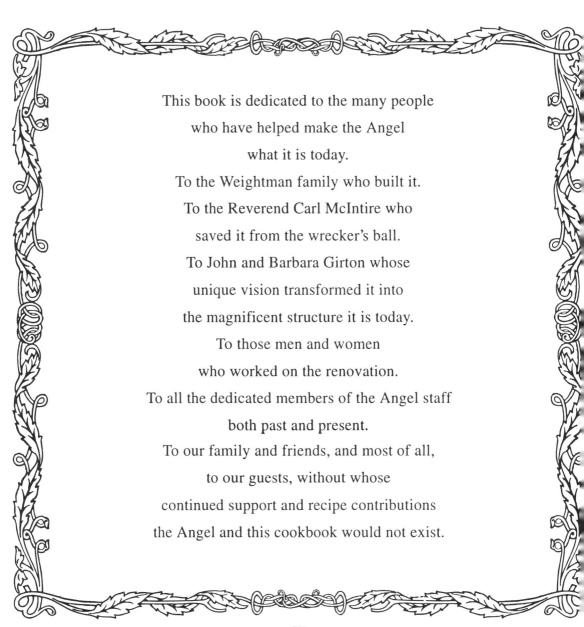

This book is dedicated to the many people
who have helped make the Angel
what it is today.
To the Weightman family who built it.
To the Reverend Carl McIntire who
saved it from the wrecker's ball.
To John and Barbara Girton whose
unique vision transformed it into
the magnificent structure it is today.
To those men and women
who worked on the renovation.
To all the dedicated members of the Angel staff
both past and present.
To our family and friends, and most of all,
to our guests, without whose
continued support and recipe contributions
the Angel and this cookbook would not exist.

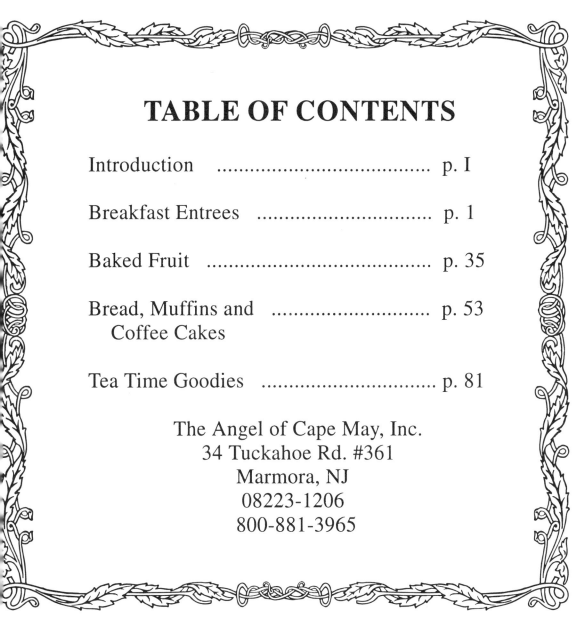

TABLE OF CONTENTS

The Angel of Cape May, Inc.
34 Tuckahoe Rd. #361
Marmora, NJ
08223-1206
800-881-3965

The Angel of the Sea was built around 1850 as a "summer cottage" for William Weightman, Sr., a Philadelphia chemist who discovered and manufactured quinine for medical applications. Built as a single structure, the house originally stood on the corner of Franklin and Washington Streets where the Cape May Post Office now stands.

In 1881, Mr. Weightman's son, William, Jr., decided that an ocean view from the broad porches of his "cottage" would be appreciated by family, friends and guests. To accomplish this goal, he hired a number of local farmers to move the house to a piece of property on the corner of Ocean and Beach Avenues, near where the Marquis de Lafayette now stands.

The farmers discovered the house was too large to move as one unit. Not wanting to lose the winter work, they decided to cut the house in half, move it in sections and then reconnect it after the move. Their task took all winter long, pulling the sections on rolling tree trunks with mule and horse power! Unfortunately, after both halves of the house were moved to the new location, the farmers discovered that, although their mules and horses were quite adequate for "pulling" the house, they proved totally ineffective in "pushing" it back together.

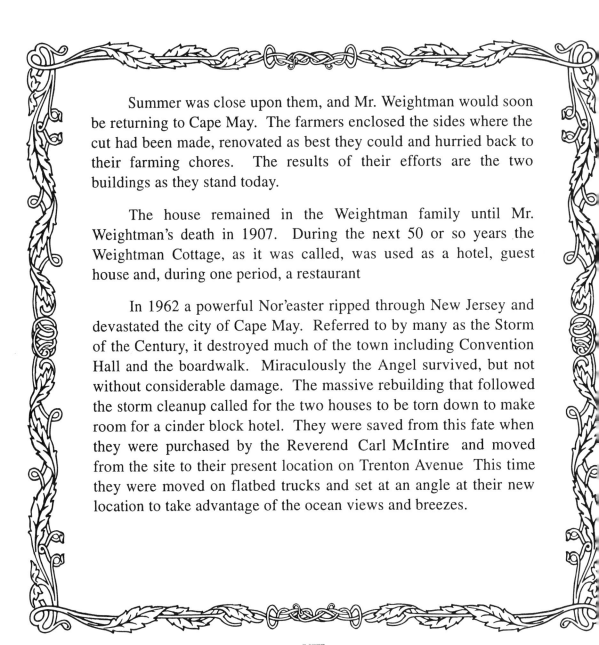

Summer was close upon them, and Mr. Weightman would soon be returning to Cape May. The farmers enclosed the sides where the cut had been made, renovated as best they could and hurried back to their farming chores. The results of their efforts are the two buildings as they stand today.

The house remained in the Weightman family until Mr. Weightman's death in 1907. During the next 50 or so years the Weightman Cottage, as it was called, was used as a hotel, guest house and, during one period, a restaurant

In 1962 a powerful Nor'easter ripped through New Jersey and devastated the city of Cape May. Referred to by many as the Storm of the Century, it destroyed much of the town including Convention Hall and the boardwalk. Miraculously the Angel survived, but not without considerable damage. The massive rebuilding that followed the storm cleanup called for the two houses to be torn down to make room for a cinder block hotel. They were saved from this fate when they were purchased by the Reverend Carl McIntire and moved from the site to their present location on Trenton Avenue This time they were moved on flatbed trucks and set at an angle at their new location to take advantage of the ocean views and breezes.

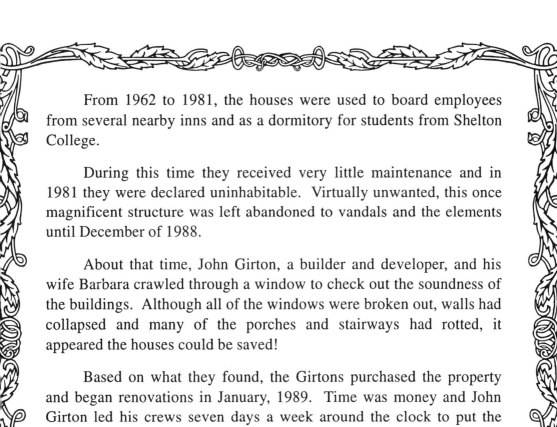

From 1962 to 1981, the houses were used to board employees from several nearby inns and as a dormitory for students from Shelton College.

During this time they received very little maintenance and in 1981 they were declared uninhabitable. Virtually unwanted, this once magnificent structure was left abandoned to vandals and the elements until December of 1988.

About that time, John Girton, a builder and developer, and his wife Barbara crawled through a window to check out the soundness of the buildings. Although all of the windows were broken out, walls had collapsed and many of the porches and stairways had rotted, it appeared the houses could be saved!

Based on what they found, the Girtons purchased the property and began renovations in January, 1989. Time was money and John Girton led his crews seven days a week around the clock to put the Angel back together. At times, as many as 75 people were working on the site during a 24 hour period. At the end of one shift, one painting crew would get off the scaffolding and another would get on it.

A trailer set up in the backyard housed a fully functional cabinet-making shop. There artisans and carpenters would find bits and pieces of the original building and piece them together. They then recreated on-site all the gingerbread detail, wall brackets and windows, copying the original designs they found.

The first of the two buildings opened in July of 1989, only six short months after renovations had begun! One year later, the most complete Victorian restoration in New Jersey was completed. The total project cost approximately $3.5 million and was done with over 103,000 man hours of labor.

After its first two successful seasons as a bed and breakfast, the Angel of the Sea was acknowledged as one of the Top Ten B & Bs in the United States by two national bed and breakfast organizations. It also won the Historic Preservation Award from the National Trust for Historic Preservation in Washington, DC for renovation to historic specifications.

Numerous local and national awards have followed and today the Angel is still rated as one of the Top Ten B & Bs in the country. It enjoys a near one hundred percent occupancy most of the year, making it necessary to book reservations months in advance.

Open year around, the Angel of the Sea is Cape May's largest and most elegant bed and breakfast. Each guest room is uniquely furnished and decorated, most have ocean views, and all, of course, have private baths. In addition, all guests have access to the Angel's many porches and verandas. Although well-behaved children over the age of eight are permitted at the Inn, they are seldom present, making the Angel a perfect destination for honeymooners, couples celebrating a special anniversary, or those just looking for a quiet, romantic getaway for two.

Mornings at the Angel begin with a hearty, sumptuous, full breakfast. Guests can help themselves to a buffet of fresh fruits, cold juices, a variety of cereals, mouth-watering, freshly baked muffins and coffee cakes, a wide assortment of teas and one of the Angel's many popular hot fruit dishes. Guests then choose one of two gourmet entrees which are served piping hot to their table.

Tea is a high point at the Angel and is served every afternoon from 4 to 5 p.m. In the warmer months guests are invited to retire with their goodies to the porches and verandas to enjoy the cool ocean breezes and panoramic views of the Atlantic. In the winter, tea time is an opportunity for guests to gather in the parlor and enjoy each other's company in front of the blazing fireplace.

Wine and cheese is served each evening from 5:30 to 7 p.m. and gives guests a chance to relax and prepare their palates for dinner at one of the many wonderful local eateries. Five of the top ten restaurants in New Jersey are located in Cape May just minutes from the Angel.

From early spring through the tranquil, late fall, bicycles are made available to guests so they can explore the island. In the summer, sand chairs, towels, umbrellas and beach tags are all provided at no charge.

So whether you choose to come in the summer to enjoy the sand and surf of the nearby beaches, or prefer to visit in the off-season to relax and experience the charm and history of Cape May, your stay at the Angel of the Sea will be an unforgettable experience, one filled with good friends, good food and cherished memories that will last a lifetime.

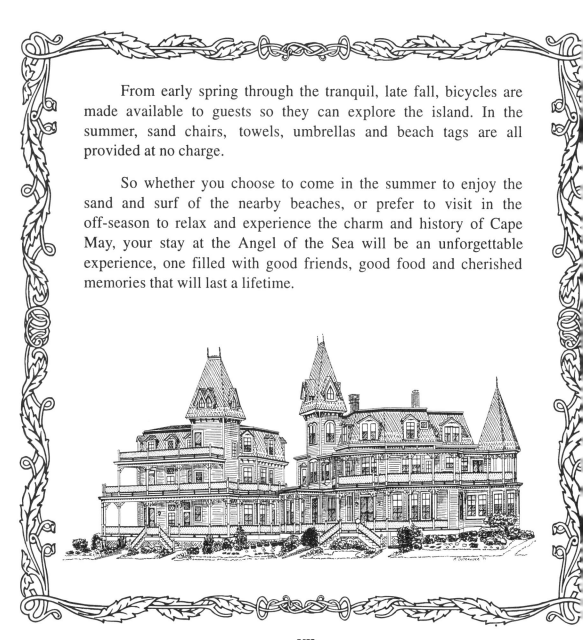

BREAKFAST ENTREES

Our guests are offered a choice
of two hot entrees each morning,
usually an egg dish
and one that is batter based,
such as pancakes, waffles or
French toast.
The following selections are just a few
of the mouth-watering dishes
that have made our breakfasts
among the largest and heartiest
in Cape May.

BACON PIE

Ingredients:

1 lb bacon fried and crumbled

1/3 cup chopped onion

2 cups Bisquick baking mix

1/2 tsp salt

2 cups shredded Swiss

4 cups milk

8 eggs

1/4 tsp pepper

Instructions:

Lightly grease two 10 inch pie plates. Sprinkle bacon, cheese and onion evenly into two dishes. Beat the remaining ingredients until smooth. Pour mixture evenly into the dishes. Bake both at 400 degrees for about 30 minutes or until the tops are golden brown. Let plates stand for five minutes before cutting. We like to serve fresh sliced garden tomatoes with this simple quiche type pie.

serves 8

FARMER'S BREAKFAST

Ingredients:

6 slices bacon - cut into one inch pieces

1 small green pepper, chopped

2 Tbs chopped onion

salt and pepper

1/2 cup shredded cheddar cheese

3 large potatoes, cooked, and cubed

6 eggs

Instructions:

Preheat oven to 375 degrees. Fry bacon in pan until crisp. Drain and set aside bacon, reserving 3 tbs of drippings. Return drippings to pan and add pepper, onions and potatoes. Cook five minutes or until brown. Sprinkle cheese over potatoes and stir until cheese melts. In separate bowl beat eggs and pour over potato mixture. Cook over low heat stirring gently. Season with salt and pepper. Pour mixture into greased casserole dish, crumble bacon over the top and bake for 45 minutes.

serves 6

GLAZED SAUSAGE & APPLES

Ingredients:

2 lbs sausage links

1/4 cup brown sugar

2 large tart apples, peeled,
cored and sliced

1/3 cup water

1 large chopped onion

Instructions:

Brown sausages. Remove from heat and drain drippings. Mix remaining ingredients and cook for 8 - 10 minutes. Stir in sausage and continue to simmer until ready to serve. Glaze thickens as it cooks and coats the sausage.

serves 8-10

ANGEL PUFF

Ingredients:

1/2 lb shredded Cheddar cheese	1/2 lb shredded Monterey Jack cheese
1 tsp baking powder	1/2 cup melted butter
1/2 tsp salt	1/2 cup flour
12 eggs	1 pint cottage cheese

Instructions:

Preheat oven to 350 degrees. Beat eggs until they are light and fluffy. Add the remaining ingredients and stir gently until well blended. Pour into a 9" x 13" baking dish. Bake for thirty minutes. For a variety try adding 1/2 lb cooked bacon, chopped Canadian bacon, chopped ham or chopped fresh broccoli. This is a great dish to be creative with.

serves 10

FRUIT KUGEL

Ingredients:

1 lb wide egg noodles	4 eggs
2 cups milk	1 cup sugar
1 lb cottage cheese	1/4 lb butter
1 pint sour cream	1 pkg dried apricots
1 medium size can crushed pineapple	

Instructions:

Preheat oven to 350 degrees. Cook and drain noodles. Mix all ingredients together. Butter a 10" x 16" baking dish. Pour the mixture into the dish. Top with crumb topping {see below} and bake at 350 degrees for one hour. Cool for 15 minutes before serving.

CRUMB TOPPING

Mix together 1 cup crushed corn flakes, 1/4 cup sugar and 2 tsp cinnamon.

serves 12.

DUTCH APPLE FRENCH TOAST

Ingredients:

3/4 cup butter	1 loaf cinnamon raisin bread
1 1/2 cups brown sugar	8 eggs
3 Tbs dark corn syrup	1 quart milk
4 apples, peeled, cored and sliced	1 1/2 tsp vanilla

Instructions:

Heat the sugar, butter and corn syrup until syrupy. Pour into a 10" x 15" pan. Spread apples over syrup. Cut the crusts off the bread and layer the slices of bread over the apples. Beat the remaining ingredients together and pour the mixture over the bread. Refrigerate overnight. Bake at 350 degrees for 45 minutes.

serves 10-12

OVEN SHIRRED EGGS

Ingredients:

6 eggs   1 cup grated cheese
12 Tbs half and half

Instructions:

Preheat oven to 450 degrees. Spray six muffin tins with non-stick spray. Break one egg in each muffin cup, pour 2 Tbs of half and half over each. Sprinkle with grated cheese. Bake at 450 degrees for 8 minutes. Be careful not to overcook. Carefully lift eggs from muffin cup with spoon. Serve over toast slices or on toasted English Muffins.

serves 3

MUSHROOM CHEESE STRATA

Ingredients:

1/2 cup butter

1 lb mushrooms, sliced

1/2 cup minced onion

1 clove garlic, minced

10 slices white bread

1/2 tsp pepper

1 cup shredded cheddar cheese

5 eggs beaten

2 3/4 cups milk

3/4 tsp salt

Instructions:

Preheat oven to 350 degrees. Melt butter in a frying pan and sauté the mushrooms, onions and garlic for 4 minutes. Lay half of the bread in the bottom of a 10" x 15" baking dish. Cover with alternating layers of cheese and mushroom mixture. Cover with the remaining bread slices. Combine eggs, milk, salt and pepper and pour over the bread. Bake at 350 degrees for 1 hour or until bread is lightly browned.

serves 10-12

BRUNCH BAKE

Ingredients:

5-8 ounces dried beef

4 cups grated sharp cheese

16 slices bread, buttered on
   one side

8 eggs beaten

1 quart milk

Instructions:

Place 8 slices of bread, buttered side down, in the bottom of a 9" x 13" baking dish. Cover with half of the dried beef and cheese. Place the remaining bread, dried beef and cheese on the top of the first layer. Beat eggs and stir together with the milk. Pour over the bread layers. Chill overnight. Bake at 300 degrees for one hour.

serves 10

EGGS BENEDICT

Ingredients:

1 stick butter, melted

3 egg yolks

1 Tbs lemon juice

6 eggs, poached

1 Tbs Grey Poupon

pinch of cayenne pepper

3 toasted English muffins

6 slices Canadian bacon

Instructions:

Sauté Canadian bacon in a small amount of water. Mix the egg yolks, lemon juice, mustard and pepper in a blender, then add the hot butter. Set mixture aside. Place one slice of bacon on half of an English muffin. Set one poached egg on top of the bacon and cover with Benedict sauce. Sprinkle the top with chopped parsley and serve immediately.

serves 3

SEAFOOD CREAM CHEESE QUICHE

Ingredients:

1 8" unbaked pie shell
stalk of celery, chopped
1/2 small onion, chopped
8 ounces cream cheese
1/4 lb grated Swiss cheese

1 lb shrimp, shelled and deveined
3 Tbs melted butter
5 large eggs
1 cup milk

Instructions:

Preheat oven to 425 degrees. Melt butter in pan and sauté shrimp, onion and celery. Cut cream cheese into 1/4 inch pieces. Cover the bottom of the pie crust with the cream cheese pieces. Add the sautéed shrimp, onion and celery and top with the grated Swiss cheese. Mix together the milk and eggs and pour over the top. Bake 10 minutes, then reduce temperature to 350 and bake for another 1/2 hour.

serves 6

EGGS MORNAY

Ingredients:

6 Tbs melted butter

6 Tbs flour

2 1/2 cups light cream

2 Tbs mustard

2 cups grated cheddar cheese

1 Tbs Worcestershire sauce

1/2 cup white wine

3 toasted English Muffins

6 eggs, poached

6 slices Canadian bacon, boiled

6 tomato slices

Instructions:

Combine flour and butter in a pot over low heat. In a separate sauce pan heat but do not boil cream. Gradually add cream to flour mixture. Stir in mustard, Worcestershire, wine, salt and pepper. Set sauce aside. Place one slice of Canadian bacon on 1/2 of an English Muffin. Place a tomato slice on top of bacon and an egg on top of the tomato. Top with the Mornay sauce.

serves 3

ZUCCHINI QUICHE

Ingredients:

1 unbaked deep pastry shell

1/2 Tbs minced fresh chives

1/4 tsp pepper

2 large eggs, beaten

3/4 cup grated cheddar cheese

bread crumbs

2 small zucchini

1 Tbs butter

1 tsp salt

2 cups sour cream

1/2 tsp baking powder

1/4 cup grated Parmesan cheese

Instructions:

Preheat oven to 400 degrees. Prick pastry shell all over with fork and bake for eight minutes or until brown. Remove from oven to cool. Reduce oven to 325 degrees.

Cut zucchini into thin slices. Melt butter in pan and sauté zucchini, chives, salt, pepper and oregano about one minute. Mix together sour cream, eggs and baking powder. Cover the bottom of the pastry shell with a layer of the zucchini mixture. Cover with layer of sour cream mixture. Alternate layers until shell is filled. Bake for 40-45 minutes or until brown and firm.

serves 8

TOMATO BACON PUFF

Ingredients:

1 lb bacon

1 can refrig. crescent rolls

2 medium tomatoes, sliced

6-8 slices Provolone cheese

3 eggs, separated

1/2 cup flour

salt and pepper

chopped parsley

Instructions:

Preheat oven to 350 degrees. Fry bacon in pan until crisp. Drain and crumble bacon. Form a crust in a 9" x 12" baking pan using the crescent roll dough. Sprinkle bacon over the crust. Cover the bottom with a layer of tomatoes, then a layer of cheese slices. Beat egg whites until stiff. In a separate bowl combine egg yolks, sour cream, flour and seasonings. Fold the egg whites into the yolk mixture. Pour over the cheese. Sprinkle parsley over the top. Bake at 350 degrees for 35 to 40 minutes.

serves 8.

WHITE WINE STRATA

Ingredients:

14-16 slices dry bread
6 Tbs melted butter
1/2 lb cheddar cheese
3 cups milk
1/4 tsp pepper
1/2 cup white wine

1 chopped onion
1/2 lb smoked cheese, grated
14 eggs
1/3 tsp red pepper
1 tbs Dijon mustard

Instructions:

Grease a 9" x 13" pan. Break bread into fourths. Put the bread and onion into the pan. Spread melted butter over the bread. Beat eggs until foamy, whisk in remaining ingredients. Pour over bread. Refrigerate overnight. Bake at 325 degrees for 1 1/2 hours, covered with foil. Remove foil and bake another 10 minutes. Let stand 15 minutes before serving.

serves 10

ORANGE FRENCH TOAST

Ingredients:

6 eggs
1/3 cup Triple Sec (opt)
3 Tbs sugar
1/4 tsp salt
peel of 1 orange, grated
3-4 Tbs butter
powdered sugar

2/3 cup orange juice
1/3 cup milk
2 Tbs vanilla
1/4 tsp cinnamon
8 slices French bread
maple syrup/honey
butter

Instructions:

Beat eggs in large bowl. Add in orange juice, Triple Sec, milk, sugar, vanilla, salt, cinnamon and peel. Dip bread in mixture, coating all sides. Place bread in baking dish and cover with remaining egg mixture. Refrigerate overnight. Melt butter in large skillet. Fry bread in batches until brown {about 4 minutes each side}. Cut bread diagonally and arrange on plate. Sprinkle with powdered sugar. Serve immediately with butter and syrup or honey.

serves 4

EGGS SWITZERLAND

Ingredients:

4 eggs   2 Tbs melted butter
1/2 cup cream   1/2 tsp pepper
pinch of cayenne   2 Tbs grated cheddar cheese
2 toasted English muffins   6 slices crisp bacon

Instructions:

Melt butter with cream in skillet. Add eggs and sprinkle with pepper and cayenne. When egg whites begin to set, sprinkle with cheese. Finish cooking and place on English muffin half with some of the hot cream and butter. Serve with bacon slices.

serves 2

POTATO BREAKFAST

This recipe was given to the Girton family by their wonderful aunt, Joan Hughes.

Ingredients:

2 1/2 cups potatoes, boiled and diced

6 slices bacon, browned and crumbled

1/4 medium onion, chopped fine

1 cup Swiss or sharp cheese, grated

1/2 cup cottage cheese

5 eggs

1/2 tsp salt

4 drops hot sauce

Instructions:

Brown potatoes and onions in oil. Combine cheese, eggs and seasonings. Mix well and place in greased 9" square baking pan. Refrigerate overnight.

Heat oven to 400 degrees. Bake for 15 minutes and then at 350 degrees for 15 minutes or until eggs are set.

serves 5-6

SHRIMP & CRAB QUICHE

Ingredients:

1/2 chopped onion	2 Tbs butter
3 eggs, beaten	3/4 cup light cream
3/4 cup milk	1/2 tsp salt
1/2 tsp lemon peel	nutmeg
3.5 oz lump crab meat	3.5 oz sm. bay shrimp
1 1/2 cup grated Swiss cheese	1/4 cup sliced almonds
1 Tbs flour	1 8" unbaked pie crust

Insructions:

Preheat oven to 350 degrees. Bake pie crust for eight minutes and remove from oven. Melt butter in skillet. Saute chopped onion. Mix in a bowl the eggs, cream, milk, onions, salt, lemon peel, nutmeg, seafood, flour and grated cheese. Put the mixture into the pie crust. Bake at 350 degrees for 45 minutes.

serves 6-8

BAKED FRENCH TOAST

Ingredients:

1 loaf firm bread	10 eggs
8 oz cream cheese	1 1/2 cup half & half
1/4 cup maple syrup	8 Tbs melted butter

Instructions:

Cube bread and layer half in a 13" x 9" pan. Cut the cream cheese into small pieces and scatter it across the bread. Cover with the remaining bread cubes. Mix the eggs, half & half, syrup and melted butter together. Pour the egg mixture over the bread cubes. Press the bread cubes down to absorb the mixture. Refrigerate overnight.

In the morning, bake at 350 degrees for 40 to 50 minutes. Serve with syrup, jam or powdered sugar.

serves 6

FIVE CHEESE
SCRAMBLED EGGS

Ingredients:

2 Tbs butter

2 Tbs garlic-herb
cream cheese

1/2 cup shredded smoked
Gouda cheese

1/2 cup grated Parmesan

2 Tbs fresh chopped parsley

8 eggs, beaten

1/2 cup shredded Cheddar
cheese

1/2 cup shredded Monterey
Jack cheese

1/2 tsp black pepper

Instructions:

Melt butter in a large fry pan over low heat. Add eggs
and cook slowly, stirring and scraping them frequently.

As the eggs thicken, add in the cream cheese and continue
stirring until it melts into the eggs. Now add the remaining
cheeses and continue to stir until the cheese melts and the eggs
are firm and creamy. Season with the pepper and garnish with
the parsley.

serves 4

SPINACH CHEDDAR BAKE

Ingredients:

1 bunch spinach, washed
  and trimmed

8 eggs

1/4 cup grated Cheddar cheese

1 stick butter, softened

salt and pepper

1/4 cup heavy cream

Instructions:

In large saucepan lightly boil salted water. Add spinach leaves and boil about 30 seconds. Drain leaves and rinse well. Squeeze remaining water out of leaves.

Preheat oven to 375 degrees and bring a saucepan of water to a boil.

Butter 4-1 cup soufflé dishes with 1 Tbs of butter each. Chop the spinach and divide it between the 4 dishes. Taking care not to break the yolks, break 2 eggs into each dish. Drizzle the cream over the eggs and sprinkle them with the cheese. Put soufflé dishes in baking pan and add boiling water until it covers the bottom half of the dishes. Bake in oven about 10 minutes or until the egg whites set.

serves 4

ITALIAN EGG PIE

This recipe is one of Uncle John's favorite Sunday morning breakfasts.

Ingredients:

1 Tbs olive oil
1/2 cup chopped onion
6 eggs
6 oz mozzarella cheese
1/4 cup fresh parsley, chopped

1 medium pepper, ringed
16 oz can tomatoes
1/4 cup water
1 tsp oregano
pepperoni or sausage, cooked

Instructions:

Preheat oven to 350 degrees. Cook onions and peppers in oil (covered) for one minute. Uncover and cook another minute. Beat eggs with water until foamy. Stir in tomatoes, grated cheese, oregano, parsley, onions and pepper rings. Pour into a greased 10" pie pan. Arrange the cooked and drained sausage and pepperoni on top. Bake 20-25 minutes.

serves 6-8

ANGEL CAKES

Ingredients:

2 cups all-purpose flour
2 eggs
2 tsp baking powder
1 tsp baking soda
1/2 tsp salt

2 Tbs sugar
2 cups buttermilk
1/2 cup milk
1/4 cup butter, melted

Instructions:

In bowl combine flour, sugar, baking powder, baking soda and salt. In another bowl lightly beat the eggs, buttermilk, milk and melted butter. Add the liquid ingredients to the dry ingredients all at once, stirring until blended. Batter should be slightly lumpy.

Heat a lightly oiled griddle over medium-high heat. Pour 1/4 cup measures of the batter on the griddle, spacing them apart. When surface begins to bubble and the underside is brown, flip the pancake and cook about 2 minutes more or until the other side is browned.

This is a very versatile recipe. For a variety try adding fruits, nuts or other ingredients into the batter or right onto the pancakes.

makes 12 pancakes

DUTCH BUNNY

Ingredients:

3 eggs   1/2 cup butter, melted

3/4 cups milk   juice of 1/2 a lemon

3/4 cup all-purpose flour   confectioners' sugar

1/2 tsp salt

Instructions:

Preheat oven to 450 degrees. Beat the eggs and milk until they are well blended. Add the flour and salt, stirring the batter until it is slightly lumpy.

Set 10" pie plate in oven to melt the butter. When the butter is very hot, pour in the batter and bake for about twenty minutes or until the pancake is brown and puffed. Sprinkled with lemon juice and confectioners' sugar and cut into wedges. Serve immediately as it will deflate quickly.

serves 4

POTATO PANCAKES

Ingredients:

2 eggs, beaten
1/4 cup all-purpose flour
1 tsp salt
1/4 cup vegetable oil

4 medium Russet potatoes
1/4 cup grated onion
1/2 tsp pepper

Instructions:

Clean and peel potatoes. Shred the potatoes using the large holes in a hand grater and squeeze the shreds to remove as much liquid as possible. Combine the eggs, flour, onion, salt and pepper in a bowl. Add the potatoes to the mixture and mix well.

In a large pan, heat some of the oil over medium-high heat. Spoon onto the pan 1/4 cup portions of the batter, flattening down the potatoes as you go. Fry until the underside is brown. Flip and fry the opposite side until it is nice and brown. Drain the cakes on paper towels before serving.

makes 10 potato pancakes

ZUCCHINI-RICOTTA CASSEROLE

Ingredients:

1 small onion, diced

1/2 tsp butter

dash salt and pepper

3 eggs

1/2 cup grated Cheddar
cheese

1/2 lb zucchini, chopped

3 Tbs all-purpose flour

1/2 tsp basil

1 lb Ricotta cheese

dash nutmeg

Instructions:

Preheat oven to 375 degrees. In a skillet, sauté the onion and zucchini in the butter. Stir in the flour and add the salt, pepper and basil. Remove from the heat and add the remaining ingredients, mixing well. Pour the mixture into a 1 1/2 quart casserole dish and bake for 40 to 45 minutes.

GREAT WITH TOASTED PITA BREAD

serves 4

BREAKFAST PIZZA

This recipe comes from Bloomsburg, PA. It is a tradition in the family and has been passed along by Joan Hughs.

Ingredients:

8-oz pkg refrigerated cresent rolls

3 eggs

1 cup cheddar cheese, shredded

12 oz sausage, cooked and drained

1/4 cup milk

1 cup frozen southern style hash browns, thawed

Instructions:

Preheat oven to 375 degrees. Press dough against bottom and sides of greased 12" pizza pan, pinch seams together to form a crust. Top with sausage and hash browns. In a small bowl beat eggs with milk; pour over pizza. Sprinkle the top with cheese. Bake for 20-30 minutes or until golden brown. Cut into wedges.

serves 8

MUSHROOM FRITTATA

Ingredients:

5 Tbs butter

12 oz button mushrooms,
   cut into 1/4" slices

1/2 tsp salt

6 eggs, beaten

1 medium clove garlic, chopped

1 oz dried porcini mushrooms,
   drained and cut into thin slices

1 Tbs chopped parsley

1/4 cup Parmesan cheese

Instructions:

Preheat oven to 350 degrees. In large skillet melt 3 Tbs of butter. Add garlic and sauté for about one minute. Add button mushrooms and salt and sauté until all liquid is evaporated and mushrooms are browned and dried, about 15 minutes. During the last minute of cooking, add the porcini mushrooms and the parsley.

Combined the eggs and mushroom mixture. In a ovenproof skillet, melt the remaining butter coating the pan evenly. Add the eggs. Bake the frittata until it is firmly set, about 20 minutes.

Cut the frittata into 4 wedges on a heated serving platter and serve.

serves 4

FRITTATA RANCHERO

Ingredients:

16 oz turkey sausage {hot}
1 cup cream
1/2 tsp salt
6 slices white bread
4.5 oz can diced chilies
1 Tbs butter
sour cream
hot sauce

6 eggs
1 1/2 tsp baking powder
2 Tbs flour
pepper
1 1/2 lb grated cheddar
  cheese
avocado
tomato wedges

Instructions:

Cook sausage until pink is gone. Set aside. Whisk eggs and cream. Add baking powder, salt, flour and bread. Blend together. Add a dash of pepper. Butter a 2 qt casserole dish. Sprinkle in half of the sausage. Layer over the sausage half of the chilies and half of the cheese. Repeat the layers using the remaining sausage, chilies and cheese. Pour egg mixture over the top. Dot with butter. Bake at 350 degrees for 40-45 minutes. Let stand for 15-20 minutes. Serve with sour cream, avocado, hot sauce and tomato.

serves 4-6

BRUNCH EGG DISH

THIS RECIPE COMES FROM THE KITCHEN OF AUNT NANCY.

Ingredients:

8-12 slices bread, buttered
1/2 lb crumbled bacon
3 cups milk

4-6 slices cheese
5 eggs
1/2 tsp salt

Instructions:

Place half of the bread, buttered side down, in a greased 8" x 12" baking dish. Place the cheese slices on top of the bread layer. Place the remaining bread slices, butter side up, over the cheese layer. Sprinkle the bacon over the bread slices. Beat together the eggs, milk and salt. Pour the mixture over the bread and cheese. Refrigerate overnight.

In the morning, bake at 350 degrees for 50 to 60 minutes.

For a variety, try adding sautéed onions, peppers, ham, mushrooms or shrimp.

serves 8-10

"CHRISTMAS"
BREAKFAST CASSEROLE

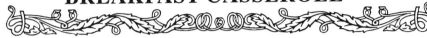

This recipe is the traditional Christmas breakfast of Linda Sallade.

Ingredients:

8 slices bread, no crusts

8 slices American cheese

3 eggs, beaten

1/4 tsp onion salt

1-1/2 cups crushed
   corn flakes

1/2 lb ham in bite size chunks

8 slices Swiss cheese

4 cups milk

1/4 tsp dry mustard

1/4 cup butter

Instructions:

Preheat oven to 400 degrees. In a 9"x 12" baking dish, layer half of the bread, then half of the ham and then the American cheese. Over the American cheese, layer the rest of the bread, the rest of the ham and then the Swiss cheese.

Mix thoroughly the eggs, milk, onion, salt and dry mustard. Pour the egg mixture over the casserole. Top the casserole off with buttered cornflakes. Bake for 40 minutes.

The casserole can be made the night before. Refrigerate it, and in the morning pour in the egg mixture, top with the cornflakes and bake.

serves 6-8

BAKED FRUIT

*Some of the most requested recipes
here at the Angel are for
our hot baked fruit,
which we serve every morning.
Interestingly enough,
the baked fruits
are the easiest things we do.*

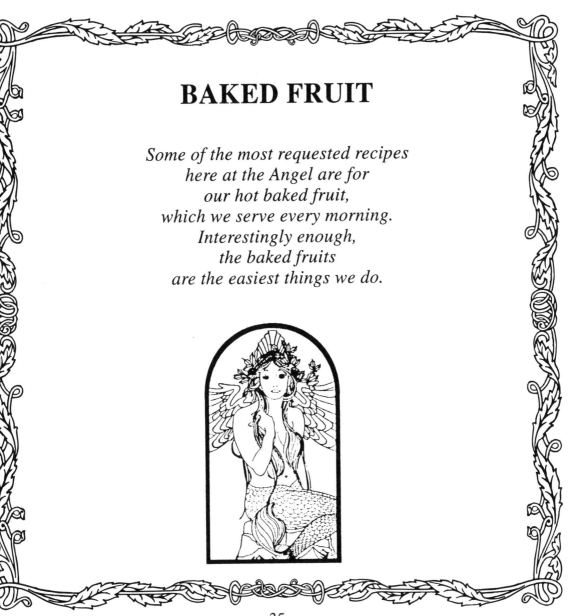

ORANGE-PINEAPPLE AMBROSIA

Ingredients:

2 cups pineapple chunks

1/2 cup coconut

1/4 cup confectioners' sugar

3 Tbs. Curacao (opt)

Pineapple sorbet

3 oranges, peeled and cut into 1/2-inch chunks

1/4 cup lime juice

18 large black cherries, pitted

Instructions:

Mix together the pineapple, oranges and coconut in a bowl. Sprinkle with the confectioners' sugar, lime juice and Curacao and toss gently. Chill 3 to 4 hours. Serve in custard cups garnished with the black cherries and the pineapple sorbet.

serves 4-6

HEAVENLY PEACHES

Ingredients:

2 20 oz cans peach halves

1 cup brown sugar

1/2 cup chopped pecans

1 cup vanilla yogurt

1/2 cup melted butter

1/2 cup oatmeal

1/2 cup granola

Instructions:

Preheat broiler to 500 degrees. Prepare the topping by combining 1/2 cup of the brown sugar, oatmeal, pecans, granola and melted butter. Mix well and set aside.

Arrange a single layer of peach halves in a shallow baking dish (rounded sides facing down). Using the remaining 1/2 cup brown sugar, place 1/2 tsp of sugar in the center of each peach. Broil for 5 minutes or until all the brown sugar has melted and been absorbed by the peaches. Remove from the broiler and place heaping spoonfuls of the topping in the center of each peach. Place under the broiler again, this time for approximately 3 minutes Be careful not to burn it! Remove from the broiler and top each peach with a tablespoon of vanilla yogurt . Serve warm.

serves 8-10

RHUBARB AND STRAWBERRY COMPOTE

Ingredients:

1/2 cup water
2" piece ginger, peeled
  and quartered
1 Tbs orange peel
1 Tbs Kirsch (optional)
heavy cream

1 cup sugar
1 lb fresh rhubarb, peeled
  and cut into 1-1/2" pieces
1 pint strawberries, hulled
  and halved

Instructions:

Bring the water, sugar and ginger to a boil in a heavy saucepan over medium heat. Add the rhubarb, bring back to boiling, then lower the heat. Partially cover and simmer for 3 to 4 minutes or until fruit is soft but retains its shape. Remove from the heat. Gently stir in the orange peel. Cool the mixture to room temperature and stir in the strawberries and Kirsch. Chill. Remove the ginger before serving. Serve topped with heavy cream.

serves 8 -10

BAKED PEARS

Ingredients:

    2 20 oz cans pear halves   1 cup fresh blueberries

    1/2 cup brown sugar   1/2 cup port wine

    nutmeg

Instructions:

Preheat the broiler to 500 degrees. Arrange a single layer of pear halves in a shallow baking dish (rounded sides facing down). Place 1/2 tsp brown sugar in the center of each pear. Broil for 5 minutes. Remove the dish from the broiler and decrease the oven temperature to 350 degrees. Pour the wine into the centers of each pear. Place 3 or 4 blueberries on each pear. Sprinkle with nutmeg. Bake in the oven for 15 minutes. Serve warm.

serves 8-10

BAKED APPLES

Ingredients:

1 tart apple, cored	2 Tbs brown sugar
1/8 tsp cinnamon	1 tsp butter
2 Tbs water	

Instructions:

Cut a few slits down the apple to prevent it from bursting. Mix in a bowl the brown sugar, cinnamon and butter. Fill the apple with the mixture. Place the apple in a oven safe baking dish and pour in the water. Bake for 20 minutes.

For more than one serving, add 2 Tbs of water and cook for an additional 10 minutes.

FRUIT COMPOTE
WITH SOUR CREAM

Ingredients:

12 oz can concentrated
   orange juice, thawed

2-1/2 Tbs cornstarch

1 cup pineapple chunks

1 cup pitted Bing cherries

2 lbs apples, peeled, sliced
   and cooked until tender

2 large bananas, sliced

1 cup cooked apricots

1/4 cup white wine

Instructions:

Preheat oven to 350 degrees. Make a paste with the orange juice and cornstarch. Lightly butter a casserole dish. In the dish, alternate layers of the fruit with layers of the orange paste, leaving the cherries for the top. Layer the top with the cherries. Cover and bake for one hour.

serves 8-10

CRANBERRY APPLE CHUTNEY

Ingredients:

1 lb fresh cranberries	1 cup water
1 cup sugar	2 green apples
1/4 cup red wine vinegar	2 Tbs lemon juice
1/3 cup sugar	1 Tbs cinnamon
1/2 tsp cloves	1 Tbs grated ginger
1/2 cup chopped walnuts	

Instructions:

In a saucepan combine the cranberries and one cup of the sugar. Bring to a boil, then reduce the heat and simmer for 10 minutes. Peel, core and cube the apples and place them in another saucepan along with the vinegar, lemon juice, 1/3 cup of sugar, cinnamon, cloves, ginger and walnuts. Lightly cook the mixture until the apples are soft. Combine the apple and cranberry mixtures and allow to cool. Refrigerate.

serves 8-10

BANANA CHANTILLY

Ingredients:

3 egg whites	3/4 cup sugar
1/2 tsp vanilla extract	1/4 tsp vinegar
1 cup mashed bananas	1/4 tsp salt
1-1/2 Tbs lemon juice	1 cup whipping cream
red cherries	

Instructions:

Preheat oven to 275 degrees. Beat egg whites until stiff. Gradually add the sugar, beating constantly. Add vanilla and vinegar. Beat until stiff and well blended. Divide the meringue in half and spread each half over a 3" x 9" baking sheet. Bake for 40 to 45 minutes or until light brown. Remove from oven and allow to cool.

Combine the banana with the salt and lemon juice. Whisk the whipped cream into the banana mixture. Remove meringues from pans. Cover one meringue with filling and top it with the second meringue. Freeze about three hours. Slice in eight portions and top with cherries.

serves 8

COCONUT BANANAS

Ingredients:

6 oz shredded coconut   1/2 cup mayonnaise

1/4 cup sweet cream   2 Tbs sugar

4 bananas, peeled

Instructions:

Heat oven to 300 degrees. Toast coconut on a cookie sheet until golden brown. Blend the mayonnaise, cream and sugar with a whisk. Cut the bananas in half and dip into the mayonnaise mixture. Roll the coated banana halves in the coconut. Arrange the bananas on a serving platter and cover with plastic wrap. Refrigerate for 30 minutes.

serves 4

CRUNCHY BAKED BANANAS

Ingredients:

2 or 3 bananas
1 Tbs butter, melted
1/2 cup miniature
   marshmallows

2 Tbs brown sugar
1 cup cornflakes

Instructions:

Preheat oven to 375 degrees. Peel the bananas and cut lengthwise. Arrange the bananas in a buttered dish. Sprinkle the brown sugar and then the marshmallows over the bananas. Mix together the melted butter and the cornflakes. Spread over the top of the banana dish. Bake for 12 to 15 minutes.

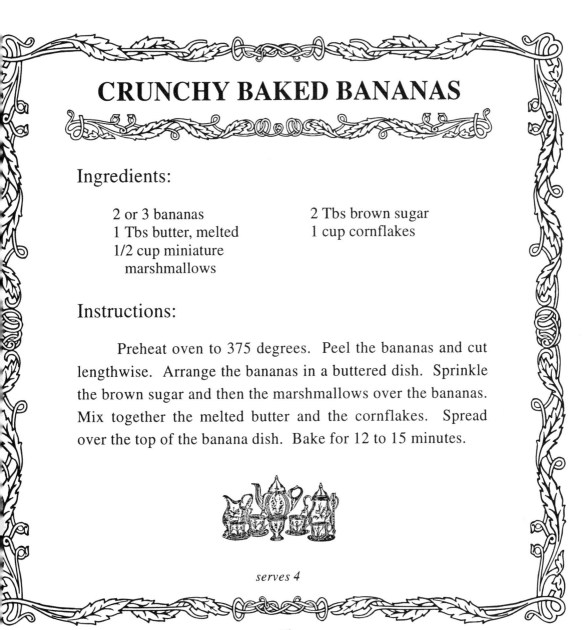

serves 4

BLUEBERRY BUCKLE

Ingredients:

1/4 cup butter, softened	3/4 cup sugar
1 egg	1 1/2 cup flour
2 tsp baking powder	1/2 tsp salt
1/2 cup milk	2 cups blueberries

TOPPING

1/2 cup sugar	1/3 cup flour
1/2 tsp cinnamon	1/4 cup butter

Instructions:

Preheat oven to 375 degrees. In a mixing bowl, cream together 1/4 cup butter, 3/4 cup sugar, and the egg. In another bowl, combine 1 1/2 cup flour, baking powder and salt. Add the flour mixture alternately with milk to the creamed mixture. Fold in the blueberries. Pour into a greased and floured 8" x 8" pan.

Prepare the topping by combining the sugar, flour, cinnamon and butter. Sprinkle over batter in the pan. Bake approximately 45 minutes. Serve warm.

serves 4-6

BLUEBERRY COBBLER

Ingredients:

1/2 cup sugar

2 Tbs water

1 cup Bisquick

1 Tbs butter, melted

1 Tbs cornstarch

4 cups blueberries

1/2 cup milk

Instructions:

Preheat oven to 350 degrees. Combine the sugar, cornstarch and water. Place blueberries in a 9" square baking dish and pour the sugar mixture over the top of them. Bake for 15 minutes.

Combine the Bisquick, milk and melted butter. Drop by tablespoons onto the hot berries and bake at 425 degrees for 15 minutes.

serves 4-6

CHERRY CRISP

Ingredients:

1/2 cup flour

1/2 cup brown sugar, packed

1 16 oz can cherry pie filling

1/3 cup pecans, chopped

1/2 cup cooking oats

1/4 cup butter, softened

1/2 tsp almond extract

Instructions:

Preheat oven to 375 degrees. Combine the flour, oats and brown sugar. Blend in the softened butter. Pat half of the mixture into the bottom of a 9" square pan. Combine the cherry pie filling and the almond extract. Spread the cherry mixture over the crust. Add the pecans to the remaining flour-oatmeal mixture and spread it over the top of the pie. Bake approximately 30 minutes. Let cool before serving.

serves 4-6

PEACH CRISP

Ingredients:

1 29-oz can sliced peaches
  (do not drain)

1 18-oz box yellow cake mix

1 cup pecans, chopped

1/2 cup butter, melted

1 cup shredded coconut

1 cup vanilla yogurt

Instructions:

Preheat oven to 325 degrees. Place the peaches along with the juice in the bottom of a 9" x 13" baking pan. Sprinkle the cake mix over the top of the peaches. Pour the melted butter over the top of the cake min. Combine the coconut and pecans, and sprinkle the mixture over the top. Bake for one hour. Top with dollops of vanilla yogurt. Serve warm.

serves 12

DIVINE PEARS
IN RASPBERRY SAUCE

Ingredients:

6 firm pears

1/4 cup lemon juice

1/2 cup orange juice

1/3 cup confectioners'
sugar, sifted

4 cups water

1 cup raspberries

2 Tbs lime juice

Instructions:

Peel pears and cut a thin slice off the bottom so that they will stand upright. Place pears in a large saucepan and add water and lemon juice. Bring to a boil, lower heat and simmer for 15 minutes. Drain. Place in a baking dish and chill for several hours.

Prepare the sauce by blending raspberries, orange juice, lime juice and confectioners' sugar in a food processor for thirty seconds. Place pears in individual serving dishes and serve with the raspberry sauce poured over.

serves 6

ANGELIC BANANAS

This recipe was created by Lorie Whissel. It's rich, quick and sooo delicious.

Ingredients:

6 bananas   3/4 cup brown sugar
1/2 cup butter, melted   1 cup sour cream.

Instructions:

Preheat oven to 375 degrees. Peel bananas and cut into 1/2" slices. Place the bananas in a shallow baking dish or a glass pie dish. Sprinkle brown sugar evenly over the top of the bananas. Pour the butter over the top. Bake for 20 to 30 minutes, gently stir with a wooden spoon after 10 minutes. Remove from the oven and spread sour cream on the top. Serve warm.

For a delicious variation, we often substitute 3 cups fresh or frozen blueberries in place of the bananas and top with yogurt instead of sour cream.

serves 6

BREADS, MUFFINS AND COFFEE CAKES

*Breakfast at the Angel is
the time for guests to
meet and mingle.
The buffet table is always
loaded with fresh cut fruits,
cereals, juices and
mouth-watering baked goods.
Here are just a few of our
guests' favorites.*

ZUCCHINI BREAD

Ingredients:

3/4 cup raisins

1/2 cup packed light
   brown sugar

3/4 tsp ground nutmeg

2 large eggs,
   at room temperature

2 cups coarsely chopped
   Zucchini

2 cups flour

1 Tbs baking powder

1 tsp salt

1/3 cup vegetable oil

1/2 cup buttermilk,
   at room temperature

1/2 cup finely chopped walnuts

Instructions:

Preheat oven to 350 degrees. Mix in a bowl the raisins and 2 Tbs of the flour. In another bowl stir together the rest of the flour, brown sugar, baking powder, salt, nutmeg and walnuts. In yet another bowl, beat the eggs with the buttermilk and oil. Stir in the zucchini and raisins.

Make a well in the center of the dry ingredients, add the buttermilk mixture and blend well. Spread the batter into a 9" x 5" greased loaf pan. Bake for one hour or until a toothpick inserted into the center of the bread comes out clean. Remove the pan to a wire rack. Cool for ten minutes before taking the bread out of the pan. Cool completely on wire rack.

makes 1 loaf

GRAPE BREAD

This is a delicious, rich, moist bread that was introduced to us by Susan Binley from the wine country of New York.

Ingredients:

3 large eggs
1 cup oil
2 tsp vanilla
3 cups flour
3 cups seeded Concord grapes

3 cups brown sugar
1 tsp cinnamon
1 tsp salt
3/4 tsp baking soda
3/4 cup chopped walnuts

Instructions:

Preheat oven to 325 degrees. Beat eggs, sugar, oil and vanilla until light in color. Mix dry ingredients together and fold the dry mixture into the egg mixture until moist--Do not beat. Gently fold in grape skins and nuts. Pour into two greased and floured bread pans. Bake for one hour or until it tests done in the center with a toothpick. Gently remove from pans and cool.

makes 2 loaves

STREUSEL RASPBERRY MUFFINS

Ingredients:

1-1/2 cups flour

2 tsp baking powder

1/2 cup butter, melted

1-1/2 cup fresh raspberries

1/2 cup sugar

1/2 cup milk

1 egg

TOPPING

1/4 cup walnuts, chopped

1/4 cup flour

1/4 cup brown sugar

2 Tbs butter, melted

Instructions:

Preheat oven to 400 degrees. In a large bowl mix flour, sugar and baking powder. In a smaller bowl combine milk, butter and egg, stir into the dry ingredients and mix until moist. Spoon half of the batter into greased and floured muffin pans. Divide raspberries evenly in muffin pans. Top each with the remaining batter. Thoroughly mix together the topping ingredients. Sprinkle the crumb topping evenly on top and bake 25-30 minutes. Delicious served warm.

makes 12 muffins

APPLE CAKE

Mable Girton, from Bloomsburg, PA, passed this recipe down to all the kitchens of the Girton family.

Ingredients:

4 cups apples, chopped fine
3/4 cup oil
1/2 tsp baking soda
1 tsp vanilla
2 eggs

2 cups sugar
2 cups flour
1 tsp cinnamon
1 tsp black walnut flavoring

TOPPING
1/2 cup brown sugar
3 Tbs butter, softened

1 Tbs flour

Instructions:

Preheat oven to 350 degrees. Combine the apples, sugar and oil. Add the rest of the ingredients and mix well. Pour into a 9" x 13" greased baking dish. Combine the topping ingredients, mixing well, and sprinkle over the top of the batter. Bake 35-40 minutes. When done baking, sprinkle with confectioners sugar or whipped cream.

serves 8

RHUBARB NUT BREAD

Ingredients:

1-1/2 cup brown sugar
1 egg, beaten
1 tsp baking soda
1 tsp vanilla
1-1/2 cup rhubarb, cut into
    small pieces

2/3 cup vegetable oil
1 cup buttermilk
1 tsp salt
2-1/2 cup flour
1/2 cup chopped walnuts

TOPPING

1 Tbs butter

1/3 cup sugar

Instructions:

Preheat oven to 350 degrees. Combine brown sugar, oil and beaten egg. In a small bowl mix together milk, baking soda, salt and vanilla. Add milk mixture to sugar mixture alternately with flour, beating well after each addition. Fold in rhubarb and nuts. Turn into 2 greased and floured 8" x 4"x 3" loaf pans. Mix topping ingredients and sprinkle on top of loaves. Bake about one hour or until toothpick inserted in center of bread comes out clean.

serves 10-12

MARIA'S BROWN SODA BREAD

Ingredients:

1 1/4 lb. whole meal flour

1 1/2 tsp baking soda

1 pint milk

3/4 lb. plain flour

1 1/2 tsp salt

3 tsp cream of tartar

Instructions:

Preheat oven to 350 degrees. Sift the white flour, soda, cream of tartar and salt into a bowl. Lightly mix in the meal flour by allowing it to sift through your fingers. Pour the milk into a well in the center of the mixture, and mix with a knife blade until most of the flour is taken up. Now knead with floured hands, adding more milk if necessary. The dough should be rather soft. Shape the dough into a round flattish cake, about 9" across and place on a floured baking tin. Cut a cross on top to allow for rising and bake for one hour or more, covering with foil about half way through cooking time so that it does not get too brown. When bread is done, it will have a hollow sound if you rap your knuckles against the bottom in the way countless Irish women have tested their "cakes" for generations! Give the bread time to get quite cold before cutting it. It will crumble badly if cut too soon.

serves 8-10

CRANBERRY NUT BREAD

Ingredients:

1 orange	1 large egg
1 cup chopped cranberries	2 cups flour
1/2 tsp salt	1/2 tsp baking soda
1-1/2 tsp baking powder	1 cup sugar
2 Tbs cold butter	1 cup chopped pecans

Instructions:

Preheat oven to 350 degrees. Using a sharp knife scrape the colored rind from the orange and mix it with the cranberries. Squeeze the juice of the orange into a measuring cup and add enough water to make 3/4 cup. Beat the egg and add it to the juice. Mix together the flour, salt, baking powder, soda and sugar in a large bowl. Cut the butter into the dry ingredients, mixing with two knives until crumbly.

Pour the juice into the dry ingredients and stir just until combined. Gently fold in the cranberries and nuts. Pour the batter into a greased 9" x 5" loaf pan. Bake for 45 to 50 minutes or until a toothpick inserted in the center comes out clean. Let cool for 10 minutes in the pan and then remove from the pan and cool completely.

serves 6-8

BLUEBERRY CRUMB MUFFINS

Ingredients:

2 cups flour
1/2 cup sugar
1 cup milk
1-1/2 cup blueberries

3 tsp baking powder
1 egg
1/4 cup oil

CRUMB MIXTURE
1/2 cup flour
1/3 cup brown sugar

1/2 tsp cinnamon
1/4 cup butter

Instructions:

Preheat oven to 400 degrees. Mix dry ingredients together in a large bowl. Combine milk, egg and oil and add to the dry ingredients. Beat slightly to moisten Do not over mix. Fill greased and floured muffin cups half full and sprinkle tops with crumb mixture. Bake for 20 minutes.

To prepare crumb mixture combine the dry ingredients, cut in butter until coarse consistency.

makes 12 muffins

GLAZED STRAWBERRY LEMON MUFFINS

Ingredients:

1-1/2 cups flour	1/2 cup sugar
2 tsp baking powder	1-1/2 tsp cinnamon
1/4 tsp salt	1/2 cup milk
1/2 cup butter, melted	1 egg
1 tsp grated lemon peel	1-1/2 cups fresh strawberries, cut into small pieces

TOPPING

1/2 cup pecans, chopped	1/2 cup brown sugar
1/4 cup flour	1-1/2 tsp cinnamon
1-1/2 tsp grated lemon peel	2 Tbs butter, melted

GLAZE

1/2 cup confectioners' sugar	1 Tbs lemon juice

Instructions:

Preheat oven to 375 degrees. In a large bowl, mix the flour, sugar, baking powder, cinnamon and salt. In another bowl, combine milk, butter and egg. Pour liquids into flour mixture and stir until moist. Fold in strawberries and lemon peel. Spoon batter into greased and floured muffin pans. Mix topping ingredients together thoroughly and spoon over batter. Bake for 20-25 minutes. Cool muffins for five minutes. Mix glaze ingredients and drizzle over the top of each muffin.

makes 12

PEACHY PECAN MUFFINS

Ingredients:

1-1/2 cups flour
2 tsp baking powder
1/4 tsp salt
1/4 cup milk
2 medium peaches,
    diced to equal one cup

1/2 cup sugar
1-1/2 tsp cinnamon
1/2 cup butter, melted
1 egg

TOPPING
1/2 cup pecans, chopped
1/4 cup flour
2 Tbs butter, melted

1/2 cup brown sugar
1-1/2 tsp cinnamon

Instructions:

Preheat oven to 400 degrees. In a large bowl, combine the flour, sugar, baking powder, cinnamon and salt. Mix butter, milk and egg together and pour into the flour mixture. Fold in peaches. Spoon mixture into greased and floured muffin pans. Combine topping ingredients and sprinkle over batter. Bake for 20-25 minutes.

makes 12 muffins

JEWISH APPLE CAKE

Ingredients:

3 cups flour	3 tsp baking powder
1 tsp salt	2 tsp grated orange peel
4 eggs	2 cups sugar
1 cup oil	1/2 cup orange juice
2 1/2 tsp vanilla	4 apples, peeled and sliced

FILLING/TOPPING
1/2 cup brown sugar   3 tsp cinnamon
1/2 cup chopped nuts or raisins

Instructions:

Preheat oven to 325 degrees. Cream the eggs and sugar together, add the oil, orange juice and orange peel. In another bowl combine the dry ingredients. Gradually mix dry ingredients into the first mixture. Pour 2 cups of the batter into a greased and floured tube pan. Layer 1/2 of the sliced apples on the batter. Sprinkle with 1/3 of filling mixture. Pour two more cups of batter into pan. Place remaining apples on batter and sprinkle with 1/3 of filling mixture. Pour remaining batter into the pan and sprinkle top with remaining filling mixture. Bake for one hour or until toothpick inserted into the center comes out clean. *serves 10-12*

BANANA OAT MUFFINS

Ingredients:

1-1/2 cups oat bran	1 cup flour
1/2 cup sugar	3 tsp baking powder
1/2 tsp salt	1 tsp non-fat dry milk
1/2 cup walnuts, chopped	2 egg whites
1 cup skim milk	1 Tbs lemon juice
1/4 cup corn oil	1 tsp vanilla
2 ripe bananas, mashed	

Instructions:

Preheat oven to 400 degrees. In a large bowl, mix together the dry ingredients. In another bowl, beat egg whites then mix in the rest of the wet ingredients. Mix the dry ingredients with the wet ingredients only until moistened. Batter will be lumpy. Spoon batter into greased and floured muffin pans and bake 20-25 minutes.

makes 12 muffins

SOUR CREAM COFFEE CAKE

Ingredients:

1/2 cup butter, softened
2 large eggs
2 cups flour
1-1/2 tsp baking powder
1 cup sour cream

1 cup sugar
1 tsp vanilla
1 tsp baking soda
1 tsp salt

FILLING
1/2 cup chopped nuts
2 tsp cinnamon

1/2 cup brown sugar

Instructions:

Preheat oven to 375 degrees. Cream butter, add sugar, eggs and vanilla. Mix dry ingredients together and add to egg mixture alternately with sour cream. Pour half of the batter into a greased and floured tube pan. Sprinkle half the filling over the batter. Pour remaining batter on filling and sprinkle with the remaining filling mixture. Bake for 35-45 minutes.

serves 10-12

BANANA CHOCOLATE CHIP MUFFINS

Ingredients:

2 extra ripe bananas	2 eggs
1 cup packed brown sugar	1/2 cup butter, melted
1 tsp vanilla	2-1/4 cups flour
2 tsp baking powder	1 tsp cinnamon
1/2 tsp salt	1 cup mini chocolate chips
1/2 cup walnuts, chopped	

Instructions:

Preheat oven to 350 degrees. Peel bananas and mash to make one cup. (The riper the bananas, the better the flavor.) In a bowl, beat the mashed bananas, eggs, sugar, butter and vanilla until well blended. In a larger bowl, combine flour, baking powder, cinnamon and salt. Stir in chocolate chips and nuts. Make a well in the center of the dry ingredients. Pour in the banana mixture. Mix until just blended. Spoon into greased and floured muffin pans. Bake for 25-30 minutes.

makes 12 muffins

EASY PINEAPPLE CAKE

Ingredients:

2 cups flour   2 cups sugar
2 eggs   2 tsp baking powder
2 tsp vanilla   1 cup chopped nuts
1 (16 oz) can crushed pineapple

FROSTING
1 8 oz package cream cheese   1/2 cup butter
2 tsp vanilla   2 cups confectioners' sugar

Instructions:

Preheat oven to 350 degrees. Mix together all cake ingredients (including juice from the pineapple) in a large mixing bowl. Bake in a greased and floured 9"x13" pan for 45 minutes. Let cool completely.

Prepare frosting by combining all the frosting ingredients and blending well. Frost the top of the cake.

serves 10-12

OLD-FASHIONED POUND CAKE

Ingredients:

3 sticks butter	3 cups sugar
5 eggs	3 cups flour
1/2 tsp baking powder	1/2 cup milk
2 tsp flavoring*	

Instructions:

Preheat oven to 350 degrees. Cream the butter and sugar. Add the eggs and beat well. Add the flour and baking powder alternately with the milk and the flavoring. Bake in a greased and floured loaf pan for 1 1/4 hours.

*Flavoring can be any of the following;
    2 tsp vanilla
    1 tsp vanilla and 1 tsp lemon
    orange flavoring
    almond flavoring

serves 8-10

ANGEL FLAKE CAKE

Ingredients:

1 pkg white or yellow
  cake mix

4 eggs

1/4 cup oil

1-1/4 cups chopped pecans

4 oz pkg vanilla instant pudding

1-1/3 cups water

1 tsp vanilla extract

1-1/2 cups coconut

Instructions:

Preheat oven to 325 degrees. Mix together the cake mix, instant pudding mix, water, eggs, vanilla and oil until well blended. Stir in the coconut and the pecans. Pour into a greased and floured tube pan and bake for one hour. Cool in pan for 15 minutes. Remove from pan and finish cooling on wire rack. Top with powdered sugar or drizzle with a glaze if desired.

serves 12

POPPYSEED CAKE

Ingredients:

3 cups flour	1/2 tsp salt
1-1/2 tsp baking soda	2 cups granulated sugar
1-1/2 cups vegetable oil	4 eggs
1 can evaporated milk	1 tsp vanilla extract
1 oz jar poppyseed	1 cup chopped nuts

Instructions:

Preheat oven to 350 degrees. Sift the dry ingredients together. Add all of the liquid ingredients and mix until smooth. Add the poppyseeds and nuts. Pour into a greased and floured tube pan. Bake for 60 minutes or until a toothpick inserted into the center comes out clean. Top with powdered sugar or drizzle with a glaze if desired.

serves 12

COCONUT DATE BREAD

Ingredients:

1-1/3 cups shredded coconut

1 tsp baking powder

1/2 tsp salt

1/2 cup sugar

1/2 cup dried pitted dates, chopped

3/4 cup coconut milk

2 tsp baking soda

2 cups all-purpose flour

2 large eggs, beaten

1/3 cup unsalted melted butter

Instructions:

Preheat oven to 375 degrees. In a bowl, sift together the flour, baking powder, baking soda and salt. Pour the eggs and sugar into a bowl. Beat with an electric mixer. While beating, add the melted butter and coconut milk. With a spoon, stir in the shredded coconut and dates. Add the flour mixture and blend well with a wooden spoon. Pour the mixture into a greased loaf pan. Bake 35 to 45 minutes or until a toothpick inserted into the center comes out clean.

makes 1 loaf

FRENCH ORANGE CAKE

Ingredients:

1 cup butter
2 cups sugar
3 cups flour
pinch of salt
5 eggs

1 tsp vanilla extract
3 Tbs grated orange rind
1 tsp baking powder
3/4 cup milk

GLAZE
1/4 cup butter
1/3 cup orange juice

2/3 cup sugar

Instructions:

Preheat oven to 350 degrees. Cream together the butter, vanilla, sugar and orange rind. Add the eggs one at a time. In another bowl sift together the flour, baking powder and salt. Add the flour to the batter alternating with the milk. Pour into a greased and floured tube pan and bake for one hour. Combined the glaze ingredients in a sauce pan and heat until the sugar dissolves. Pour the glaze over the cake while the cake is still hot.

serves 12

JALAPENO CORNBREAD

Ingredients:

1-1/3 cups yellow cornmeal
1 Tbs baking powder
1/8 tsp cayenne pepper
1 cup sour cream
1 large egg, beaten
1/4 cup jalapeno peppers,
  seeded, finely diced

2/3 cup all-purpose flour
1 tsp salt
1 tsp ground cumin
1/3 cup half & half
1/4 cup melted butter
7 oz corn kernels, drained
1/2 cup diced scallion
  (white & light green parts)

Instructions:

Preheat oven to 425 degrees. In a bowl, sift together the cornmeal, flour, baking powder, salt, cayenne pepper and cumin. In another bowl whisk together the sour cream and half & half. Add the beaten egg and whisk in thoroughly. Whisk in the melted butter. Add the cornmeal mixture and blend well with a wooden spoon. Stir in the jalapeno peppers, corn kernels and scallion. Pour the mixture into a well greased 11" x 18" baking pan. Bake 20 to 25 minutes or until the edges are brown. Serve hot.

serves 24

RUM CAKE

Ingredients:

1 pkg yellow cake mix	4 eggs
1/2 cup oil	1 pkg vanilla instant pudding
1/2 cup water	1/2 cup light rum
chopped nuts	

GLAZE
1/2 cup butter	1 cup sugar
1/4-1/2 cup rum	

Instructions:

Preheat oven to 350 degrees. Sprinkle chopped nuts into the bottom of a greased and floured tube pan. Combined cake mix, eggs, pudding, oil, water and rum. Pour into cake pan and bake for 45 to 60 minutes.

Mix glaze ingredients in a sauce pan and bring to a boil. Cook for one minute. Pour the glaze over the cake while it is still warm. Let the cake cool in the pan for 30 minutes. Remove the cake from the pan by flipping the cake upside down on a cake plate. The chopped nuts are now on the top of the cake.

serves 12

PEAR MANGO BREAD

Ingredients:

1/4 cup butter, melted

2 tsp baking powder

1 cup mango nectar

2 large eggs

2-1/2 cups all-purpose flour

1/2 tsp salt

1/2 cup sugar

16 oz can pears, drained and chopped

Instructions:

Preheat oven to 375 degrees. In a bowl, sift together the flour, baking powder and salt. In a large bowl, mix together the melted butter, mango nectar and sugar. Beat with an electric mixer until the sugar dissolves. While beating, add the eggs one at a time. Add the flour mixture and thoroughly blend with a wooden spoon. Stir in the chopped pears. Pour into a greased and floured loaf dish. Bake 40 to 45 minutes or until a toothpick inserted into the center comes out clean.

makes 1 loaf

VICTORIAN GINGERBREAD

Ingredients:

1/2 cup butter, softened
1 tsp baking soda
2 tsp ground cinnamon
2 large eggs
1/2 Tbs grated orange rind
3/4 cup dark unsulphured
   molasses

1/2 cup sugar
1 tsp ground ginger
1/4 tsp ground nutmeg
1/2 cup orange juice
2 cups all-purpose flour

Instructions:

Preheat oven to 375 degrees. Using an electric mixer, cream the butter and sugar until the sugar is dissolved and the mixture is creamy. Pour mixture into saucepan and add the molasses. Bring to a boil stirring constantly. Stir in the baking soda, ginger, cinnamon and nutmeg. Remove from heat. In a large bowl whisk the eggs until well beaten. Whisk in the molasses mixture. Add the orange juice and beat well. Add the orange rind and whisk in the flour. Pour the mixture into a greased and floured loaf pan. Bake 25 to 35 minutes or until a toothpick inserted into the middle comes out clean.

makes 1 loaf

CINNAMON RAISIN BREAD

Ingredients:

1 large egg
1/4 cup butter, melted
2-1/2 tsp baking powder
1/4 tsp salt
1 Tbs ground cinnamon
1/2 cup dark brown sugar,
  firmly packed

1 cup buttermilk
2-1/2 cups all-purpose flour
1/2 tsp baking soda
1/2 cup sugar
1 cup seedless raisins

Instructions:

Preheat oven to 350 degrees. Beat the egg with a whisk in a large bowl. Whisk in the buttermilk and melted butter. Directly into the liquid mixture, sift in the flour, baking powder, baking soda, salt, sugar, brown sugar and cinnamon. Blend with a wooden spoon. Fold in the raisins. Pour the mixture into a greased and floured loaf pan. Bake 45 to 55 minutes or until a toothpick inserted into the center comes out clean.

makes 1 loaf

PEANUT BUTTER BREAD

Ingredients:

2 cups all-purpose flour
3/4 tsp baking soda
2 Tbs butter, melted
1 large egg, beaten
1/4 cup dark brown sugar,
   firmly packed

1 tsp baking powder
1/4 tsp salt
1/3 cup smooth peanut butter
1/4 cup seedless raisins
1/4 cup roasted, unsalted
   peanuts

Instructions:

Preheat oven to 350 degrees. In a bowl, sift together the flour, baking powder, baking soda and salt. In a separate large bowl, combine the melted butter, brown sugar and peanut butter. Beat the ingredients thoroughly with an electric mixer. Add the beaten egg and beat until smooth. Add one third of the flour mixture, continuing to beat until smooth. With a wooden spoon, stir in the peanuts, raisins and buttermilk. Add the remaining flour and blend well. Pour the mixture into a greased and floured loaf pan. Bake 45 to 55 minutes or until a toothpick inserted into the center comes out clean.

makes 1 loaf

TEA TIME GOODIES

Whether tea is for two
or fifty-two,
we always treat our guests
to traditional,
and sometimes, not so traditional
tea time goodies.

RAISIN FILLED COOKIES

THIS COOKIE RECIPE COMES FROM MABLE GIRTON. IT HAS BEEN ENJOYED HOT OUT OF THE OVEN, BY FOUR GENERATIONS OF GIRTON CHILDREN.

Ingredients:

2 cups sugar
1 cup shortening
1 tsp vanilla
4 1/2 cups flour
2 tsp baking soda

2 eggs
1 tsp salt
1 cup sour milk
1/2 tsp cream of tartar

RAISIN FILLING
1 lb of raisins, ground
3/4 cup sugar

1 cup water
4 heaping tsp of flour

Instructions:

Prepare raisin filling by combining the sugar, water and flour. Place ground raisins in a medium sauce pan. Add the flour mixture and cook until the mixture thickens. Wrap tightly and keep overnight.

Mix sugar, eggs, shortening, salt and vanilla. Add baking soda to milk and stir, it will foam up. Add the milk mixture to the first mixture. Combine the flour and cream of tartar. Add the flour mixture to the batter mixture. Refrigerate overnight to harden.

Preheat oven to 350 degrees. Roll out the dough on a floured board. Cut the dough with a two inch round cookie cutter. Place 1 circle on cookie sheet, put one tsp raisin mix on circle, and then cover with another circle of dough. You do not need to seal the edges, it will bake together. Bake approximately 20 minutes or just until slightly brown.

makes 3 to 4 dozen

ANGEL LEMON SQUARES

Ingredients:

1 can condensed milk

1 Tbs lemon peel

1 cup brown sugar

1/2 tsp baking soda

1-1/2 cup oats

1/2 cup lemon juice

2/3 cup shortening

1-3/4 cup flour

1 tsp salt

Instructions:

Preheat oven to 350 degrees. To make lemon filling, blend milk, juice and lemon peel until thick. Mix shortening and sugar together. Blend the dry ingredients, excepts oats, into the shortening to make crumb mixture. Stir in oats. Place 1/2 of the crumb mixture into a greased 9" x 13" pan, press and flatten. Spread the lemon filling on crumb crust and sprinkle the remaining crumb mixture on top. Bake for 25-30 minutes.

makes 24 bars

OLD-FASHIONED
SOUR CREAM COOKIES

Ingredients:

1 cup sugar

1/4 cup butter, softened

1 tsp vanilla

1 tsp baking powder

1/2 tsp salt

1/2 cup sour cream

1/4 cup shortening

1 egg

2-2/3 flour

1/2 tsp baking soda

1/4 tsp nutmeg

sugar

Instructions:

Preheat oven to 425 degrees. Mix 1 cup sugar, shortening, butter, egg and vanilla in a bowl. Stir in remaining ingredients. Shape dough into tablespoon size balls. Place on an ungreased cookie sheet. Flatten balls with greased bottom of a glass dipped in sugar. Bake until almost no indentation remains when touched, 6 to 8 minutes.

makes 3 dozen

ENGLISH SCONES

Ingredients:

2 cups flour	4 Tbs sugar
1/2 tsp salt	2 tsp baking powder
6 Tbs butter	2 eggs
1/2 cup sour cream	1/2 tsp vanilla

Instructions:

Preheat oven to 375 degrees. Lightly butter a baking sheet. Sift flour into a bowl with sugar, salt and baking powder. Add the butter and work with your fingers until the mixture resembles coarse meal. Combine the eggs, cream and vanilla in a bowl. Add to the flour mixture and stir until moistened. Flour your hands well. Working quickly, lightly pat the dough into an 8" round. With a sharp knife, score the round into 8 wedges. (Dough can also be rolled and cut into biscuit shapes.) Place on the baking sheet and bake for about 20 minutes until the top is browned and a toothpick inserted in the center comes out clean. Remove scones to a wire rack and cool for a few minutes. Cut along the score marks and serve warm with butter, preserves or clotted cream.

makes 8 scones

CHEWY OATMEAL BARS

Ingredients:

4 cups oats

1 cup brown sugar

1 tsp salt

3/4 cup orange marmalade

1-1/2 cups walnuts, chopped

1 cup shredded coconut

3/4 cup butter, melted

Instructions:

Preheat oven to 400 degrees. Combine all ingredients, mix well. Press into a 10" x 15" greased pan. Bake until golden brown, approximately 18-22 minutes. Cool and cut into bars.

makes 28 squares

FRUIT TARTS

Ingredients:

1/2 cup butter, softened

1 cup flour

3 oz. cream cheese, softened

1 can of your favorite pie
filling or fruit preserves

Instructions:

Preheat oven to 350 degrees. Put paper liners in mini-muffin tins. Mix butter, cream cheese and flour together and shape into balls the size of walnuts. Press the balls into mini muffin tins. Fill with pie filling. Bake at 350 degrees for 10 minutes. Reduce the heat to 250 degrees and continue baking for 15-29 more minutes.

RUSSIAN TEA CAKES

Ingredients:

1 cup butter
1 tsp vanilla
1/4 tsp salt
Additional confectioners'
  sugar for rolling cookies

1/2 cup confectioners' sugar
2-1/4 cups flour
3/4 cup chopped nuts

Instructions:

Cream butter, sugar and vanilla. Mix dry ingredients together and gradually add to the first mixture. Stir in the chopped nuts and form dough into a ball. Wrap tightly with plastic wrap and chill for at least one hour.

When ready to bake, preheat oven to 400 degrees. Remove dough from the refrigerator and roll pieces of dough into 1 inch balls. Bake on an ungreased cookie sheet 10-12 minutes. Cookies should be set but not brown. Roll cookies in confectioners' sugar while they are still warm. Cool and roll again in confectioners' sugar.

makes 2 dozen

LEMON BARS

Ingredients:

CRUST
2 cups flour
1 cup butter

1/2 cup confectioners' sugar

TOPPING
4 eggs
1/3 cup lemon juice
1/2 tsp baking powder

2 cups sugar
1/4 cup flour

Instructions:

Preheat oven to 350 degrees. Sift together flour and confectioners' sugar. Cut in butter till mixture clings together. Press into a 13"x 9" pan and bake for 20-25 minutes or until lightly browned. While crust is baking, prepare topping by beating eggs together with the sugar and lemon juice. Sift flour and baking powder together and stir into egg mixture. Pour topping over baked crust and bake for an additional 25 minutes. Sprinkle with confectioners' sugar. Let cool thoroughly before cutting into squares.

makes 24 bars

MINI CHERUB CHEESECAKES

Ingredients:

12 vanilla wafers	2 eggs
1/2 cup sugar	1 tsp vanilla
2 8 oz. packages cream cheese, softened	

Instructions:

Preheat oven to 325 degrees. Line muffin tins with foil liners. Place one vanilla wafer in the bottom of each liner. Mix cream cheese, vanilla and sugar until well blended. Add eggs and mix well. Pour mixture over the wafers, filling each tin 3/4 full. Bake for 25 minutes. Remove from pan to cool. Chill. Top with fruit, preserves or melted chocolate before serving.

serves 12

MINI DEVIL CHEESECAKES

Ingredients:

1-1/3 cups graham cracker crumbs

1/4 cup cocoa

3 8 oz. packages of cream cheese, softened

3 eggs

14 oz. sweetened condensed milk

1/3 cup sugar

1/3 cup butter, melted

2 12 oz. packages semi-sweet chocolate chips

2-1/2 tsp vanilla

Instructions:

Preheat oven to 300 degrees. Stir together crumbs, sugar, cocoa and butter. Press equal portions into paper lined muffin tins. In a small saucepan melt 1 package of chocolate chips over low heat. In mixer bowl, beat cheese until fluffy. Gradually beat in condensed milk and melted chips until smooth. Add eggs and vanilla, mixing well. Spoon batter into cups. Top with remaining chips. Bake 20 minutes or until set. Cool then refrigerate.

makes 30

HONEY OATMEAL COOKIES

Ingredients:

1-1/4 cups sugar	1/2 cup shortening
2 eggs	1/3 cup honey
1-3/4 cups flour	1 tsp baking soda
1 tsp salt	2 cups oats
1 cup raisins	1/2 cup chopped nuts

Instructions:

Preheat oven to 375 degrees. Mix sugar, shortening, eggs and honey. Stir in remaining ingredients. Drop dough by rounded teaspoonfuls onto an ungreased cookie sheet. Bake until light brown, 8-10 minutes. Immediately remove from cookie sheet.

makes 2 dozen

IRISH SCONES

Ingredients:

3 cups flour	3/4 cups sugar
2 tsp baking powder	1 tsp salt
1-1/3 cups milk	1 egg, slightly beaten
3/4 cup butter, melted	1-1/2 cups raisins

Instructions:

Preheat oven to 325 degrees. Mix dry ingredients together. Very slowly stir in milk, egg and cooled butter. Fold in raisins. Bake in a greased and floured 9" x 5" x 2" baking dish for one hour. Cut into squares and serve with butter, clotted cream or preserves.

serves 12

CREME DE MENTHE
CHOCOLATE SQUARES

Ingredients:

BROWNIES
1 cup sugar	1/2 cup butter
4 eggs, beaten	1 cup flour
1 tsp vanilla	1/4 cup chocolate syrup

CREME DE MENTHE LAYER
2 cups confectioners' sugar   1/2 cup butter, melted
3 Tbs green Creme de Menthe

GLAZE
3/4 cup chocolate chips   6 Tbs butter

Instructions:

Preheat oven to 350 degrees. Cream sugar, butter and eggs. Add flour and salt and mix well. Blend in vanilla and chocolate syrup. Pour batter into a greased 9" x 13" pan. Bake for 30 minutes. Cool in pan. While brownies are cooling, make mint layer by mixing together sugar, Creme de Menthe and butter. Spread over cooled brownies.

To make glaze, melt chocolate chips and butter together until smooth. Cool and spread thinly over mint layer. Chill until ready to serve. Cut into small squares.

makes 2 dozen

CARAMEL NUT BARS

Ingredients:

CRUST

1 cup flour	1 cup whole wheat flour
1 cup packed brown sugar	1 tsp baking soda
1/4 tsp salt	1 cup butter

TOPPING

2 cups mixed nuts, chopped	1 cup chocolate chips
1 12.5 oz. jar caramel ice cream topping	3 Tbs flour

Instructions:

Preheat oven to 350 degrees. Combine all crust ingredients except butter. Cut in butter with fingers until mixture resembles crumbs. Press evenly into a greased 9" x 13" pan. Bake for 10 minutes.

Sprinkle nuts and chocolate chips over warm crust. In a bowl combine caramel topping and flour, mixing well. Pour evenly over chocolate chips and nuts. Return to oven and bake an additional 15-18 minutes or until topping is set. Cool completely before cutting into bars.

makes 24 bars

APPLESAUCE GRANOLA BARS

Ingredients:

1/2 cup packed brown sugar   1/2 cup butter, softened

1/2 cup applesauce   2 tsp lemon peel

1 egg   1 cup whole wheat flour

1 tsp baking soda   1/4 tsp cinnamon

1 cup granola

Instructions:

Preheat oven to 350 degrees. Cream together brown sugar and butter. Add applesauce, lemon peel and egg, mix well. Combine flour, baking soda and cinnamon. Gradually add it to the butter mixture, mixing well. Stir in granola. Spread into a greased 9" square pan. Bake for 30-35 minutes. Cool completely and cut into bars.

makes 16

CHERRY WALNUT BARS

Ingredients:

CRUST
2 cups flour

1 cup butter, softened

1/2 cup sugar

TOPPING
2 eggs, slightly beaten

1-1/2 cups packed brown sugar

1/2 cup maraschino cherries, chopped

1/4 cup flour

1/2 tsp baking powder

1 cup walnuts, chopped

Instructions:

Preheat oven to 350 degrees. Combine all crust ingredients and mix well. Press into a greased 9" x 13" pan. Bake for 20 minutes or until golden brown.

To prepare topping, beat eggs and brown sugar together until fluffy. Add flour and baking powder, mix well. Stir in cherries and walnuts. Pour filling over baked crust. Return to oven and bake an additional 25-30 minutes or until filling is set.

makes 24

PINEAPPLE MACAROONS

Ingredients:

8 egg whites	1-1/3 cup sugar
1 cup flour	1/4 tsp salt
8 cups coconut	2 8 oz. cans crushed pineapple, well-drained

Instructions:

Preheat oven to 325 degrees. In large bowl, beat egg whites until stiff. Gradually add sugar, beating until stiff peaks form. Fold in flour and salt. Stir in coconut and pineapple. Drop dough by tablespoons 2 inches apart onto a well-greased cookie sheet. Bake for approximately 15 minutes or until set and lightly browned. Cool for a couple minutes before removing from cookie sheet. Cool completely before serving.

makes 4 dozen

NUT BONBON COOKIES

Ingredients:

2 cups flour	1 8 oz. package cream cheese
1/2 cup shortening	1/2 cup butter, softened
confectioners' sugar	walnut halves

Instructions:

Mix cream cheese, butter and shortening with fork. Mix in flour with hands. Chill for several hours.

Preheat oven to 375 degrees. Roll out dough 1/8" thick on cloth-covered board sprinkled with confectioners' sugar. Cut dough into 3" x 1" rectangles Put a walnut half on each rectangle and roll up. Place on a greased baking sheet with end of roll underneath. Bake 15 minutes or until golden brown. Sprinkle cookies immediately with confectioners' sugar. Serve warm if possible.

makes 4 dozen

TOFFEE SQUARES

Ingredients:

1 cup butter, softened	1 cup packed brown sugar
1 egg yolk	1 tsp vanilla
2 cups flour	1/4 tsp salt
1-1/2 cups chocolate chips	1/2 cup chopped nuts

Instructions:

Preheat oven to 350 degrees. Combine butter, sugar, egg yolk and vanilla. Blend in flour and salt. Spread dough onto a greased 9"x13" pan.   Bake 20-25 minutes or until lightly browned.   Remove from oven.   Immediately place chocolate chips on top. Let stand until chocolate is soft, spread evenly over entire surface. Sprinkle with nuts. Cut into bars while still warm.

makes 24 bars

DREAM BARS

Ingredients:

CRUST
1/4 cup shortening

1/2 cup packed brown sugar

1/4 cup butter, softened

1 cup flour

TOPPING
2 eggs, well beaten

1 tsp vanilla

1 tsp baking powder

1 cup shredded coconut

1 cup packed brown sugar

2 Tbs. flour

1/2 tsp salt

1 cup slivered almonds

Instructions:

Preheat oven to 350 degrees. Combine shortening, butter and brown sugar, mix thoroughly. Stir in flour. Press into an ungreased 9" x 13" pan. Bake for 10 minutes.

While crust is cooking, prepare topping by combining eggs, sugar and vanilla. Add flour, baking powder and salt, mixing thoroughly Stir in coconut and almonds. Spread topping onto baked crust. Return to oven and bake an additional 25 minutes or until golden brown. Cool slightly and cut into bars.

makes 24 bars

BRAZILIAN COFFEE COOKIES

Ingredients:

1/3 cup shortening	1/2 cup brown sugar
1/2 cup granulated sugar	1 egg
1-1/2 tsp vanilla	1 Tbs milk
2 cups flour	1/2 tsp salt
1/4 tsp baking soda	1/4 tsp baking powder
2 Tbs instant coffee	

Instructions:

Preheat oven to 400 degrees. In a bowl, mix the shortening, sugars, egg, vanilla and milk until fluffy. Measure flour by sifting and mix dry ingredients together. Add this to the sugar mixture and stir thoroughly. Shape dough into 1" balls. Place balls 2" apart on an ungreased baking sheet. Flatten to 1/8" thick with a greased fork dipped in sugar. Bake 8 to 10 minutes or until brown.

makes 2-3 dozen

THUMBPRINT COOKIES

Ingredients:

1/2 cup shortening
(part butter)

1/4 cup brown sugar

1/2 tsp vanilla

jelly or powdered sugar icing

3/4 cup finely chopped nuts

1/4 tsp salt

1 egg (separated)

1 cup flour

Instructions:

Preheat oven to 350 degrees. In a bowl, mix together the shortening, sugar, egg yolk and vanilla. Measure flour by sifting and stir together with the salt. Combine flour mixture with egg mixture to form dough. Roll dough into 1 tsp balls. Beat egg white slightly with fork. Dip the dough balls into the egg white and roll in the nuts. Place balls about 1" apart on a greased baking sheet and press thumb into the center of each ball. Bake 10 to 12 minutes. Cool. Fill thumbprints with jelly or powdered sugar icing.

makes 2-3 dozen

JAN HAGEL

Ingredients:

1 cup butter, softened
1 egg, separated
1/2 tsp cinnamon
1/2 cup very finely chopped
  walnuts

1 cup sugar
2 cups flour
1 Tbs water

Instructions:

Preheat oven to 350 degrees. Lightly grease a jelly roll pan. In a bowl, mix the butter, sugar and egg yolk. Measure the flour by sifting and mix with the cinnamon. Stir the flour mixture into the butter mixture. Pat the dough into the pan. Beat water and egg white until frothy. Brush the froth over the dough and sprinkle with nuts. Bake 20 to 25 minutes or until lightly brown. Cut immediately into finger-like strips.

makes 2-3 dozen

FUDGE MELT-A-WAYS

Ingredients:

3/4 cup butter

2 tsp vanilla

2-1/2 sq (oz) unsweetened chocolate

1/2 cup chopped nuts

1 Tbs milk or cream

1 cup coconut

1/4 cup granulated sugar

2 cups graham cracker crumbs

1 egg, beaten

2 cup sifted powdered sugar

Instructions:

In a saucepan, melt 1/2 cup butter and 1 square of chocolate. Blend together the granulated sugar, 1 tsp vanilla, egg, crumbs, coconut and nuts into the butter-chocolate mixture. Mix well and press into an ungreased 9" x 13" baking dish. Refrigerate.

Mix together 1/4 cup butter, milk, powdered sugar and 1 tsp vanilla. Spread over crumb mixture. Chill.

Melt 1-1/2 square of chocolate and spread over chilled filling. Chill. Cut before firm.

makes 24

ALMOND BUTTER COOKIES

Ingredients:

1 cup butter	2 tsp vanilla
1/2 cup sugar	2 cups flour
1 cup finely chopped almonds (with skin)	

Instructions:

Preheat oven to 350 degrees. Cream the butter and the sugar together. Stir in the almonds and the vanilla. Measure the flour by sifting and combine it into the mixture with a pastry blender. Form the dough into teaspoon size balls and place on an ungreased baking sheet. Flatten the balls with the bottom of a greased spoon dipped in sugar. Bake 8 to 10 minutes or until slightly brown.

makes 2-3 dozen

SPICY SUGAR DROPS

Ingredients:

2 3/4 cups flour
1 1/2 cups packed brown sugar
1 tsp salt
1/2 tsp baking soda
1 cup nuts, chopped

1 cup sour cream
1/2 cup shortening
1 tsp vanilla
2 eggs

SPICY SUGAR
1/2 cup sugar
1 tsp ground cloves

1 tsp cinnamon

Instructions:

Preheat oven to 375 degrees. Cream together sugar, shortening and eggs, add sour cream and vanilla. Mix together flour, salt and soda and gradually add to the first mixture. Stir in nuts. Drop dough by level tablespoons about two inches apart onto an ungreased cookie sheet. Sprinkle the top of each with the Spicy Sugar mixture. Bake approximately 10 minutes. Immediately remove from the cookie sheet to cool.

makes 2 1/2 dozen

(G)

(H)

(I)

(F)

(A) - (B)

(L)

(J)

(C) - (D)

(E)

(K)

(M)

ORDER CARD

Angel's most popular gifts, mail attached order card or call 1-800-881-3965 for prompt delivery.

ANGEL OF THE SEA GIFT ORDER

ORDER LINE 1-800-881-3965

	Angel of the Sea Cookbook	_____ x 14.95 = _____	
A&B	Angel of the Sea Inn Water Color Print (Front Cover) 11 x 14	_____ x 25.00 = _____	
	Signed by John & Barbara Girton and artist Ken Fry	7 x 11	_____ x 15.00 = _____
C&D	The Angel Water Color Print (Back Cover) 11 x 14	_____ x 25.00 = _____	
	Signed by John & Barbara Girton and artist V. Mae Townsend	7 x 11	_____ x 15.00 = _____
E	Angel of the Sea Ceramic Plaque (9"W x 8"H x 2" Deep)	_____ x 69.95 = _____	
	Brian Bakers "De Ja Vu" Collection, Signed by John & Barbara Girton		

F Angel Embroidered Sweat Shirt ___ S ___ M ___ L ___XL .... _____ x 59.95 = _____
Qty Qty Qty Qty

___ XXL ___ XXXL .... _____ x 69.95 = _____
Qty Qty

G Inn Embroidered Sweat Shirt ___ S ___ M ___ L ___ XL .... _____ x 59.95 = _____
Qty Qty Qty Qty

___ XXL ___XXXL .... _____ x 69.95 = _____
Qty Qty

H Angel Sweat Shirt-Printed ___ S ___ M ___ L ___ XL .... _____ x 29.95 = _____
Qty Qty Qty Qty

___ XXL ___ XXXL .... _____ x 39.95 = _____
Qty Qty

I Angel T-Shirt-Printed ___ S ___ M ___ L ___XL .... _____ x 15.00 = _____
Qty Qty Qty Qty

J Angel Tank Top-Printed ___ S ___ M ___ L ___ XL .... _____ x 15.00 = _____
Qty Qty Qty Qty

K Angel Mugs .... _____ x 12.00 = _____

L Angel of the Sea Miniature (3" x 3" x 3") .... _____ x 15.00 = _____

M Cape May Light House Miniature (3" x 3" x 4" High) .... _____ x 15.00 = _____

Sub Total = _____

Shipping & Handling 3.00 per item = _____

NJ Residents Add 6% Sales Tax = _____

Total = _____

Name: _____

Address: _____

_____

Phone: _____-_____-_____

Credit Card: ____ Visa ____ Master Card   Exp. date: _____

Card#: _____

Signature: _____

Prices Subject to Change Without Notice

The Angel of Cape May, Inc.
34 Tuckahoe Rd. #361
Marmora, NJ 08223-1206

ORDER CARD

Angel's most popular gifts, mail attached order card or call 1-800-881-3965 for prompt delivery.

ANGEL OF THE SEA GIFT ORDER

ORDER LINE 1-800-881-3965

	Angel of the Sea Cookbook		_____ x 14.95 =	_____
A&B	Angel of the Sea Inn Water Color Print (Front Cover) 11 x 14..................		_____ x 25.00 =	_____
	Signed by John & Barbara Girton and artist Ken Fry	7 x 11	_____ x 15.00 =	_____
C&D	The Angel Water Color Print (Back Cover) 11 x 14		_____ x 25.00 =	_____
	Signed by John & Barbara Girton and artist V. Mae Townsend	7 x 11	_____ x 15.00 =	_____
E	Angel of the Sea Ceramic Plaque (9"W x 8"H x 2" Deep)		_____ x 69.95 =	_____
	Brian Bakers "De Ja Vu" Collection, Signed by John & Barbara Girton			
F	Angel Embroidered Sweat Shirt ___ S ___ M ___ L ___XL		_____ x 59.95 =	_____
	Qty Qty Qty Qty ___ XXL ___ XXXL		_____ x 69.95 =	_____
	Qty Qty			
G	Inn Embroidered Sweat Shirt ___ S ___ M ___ L ___ XL		_____ x 59.95 =	_____
	Qty Qty Qty Qty ___ XXL ___XXXL		_____ x 69.95 =	_____
	Qty Qty			
H	Angel Sweat Shirt-Printed ___ S ___ M ___ L ___ XL		_____ x 29.95 =	_____
	Qty Qty Qty Qty ___ XXL ___ XXXL		_____ x 39.95 =	_____
	Qty Qty			
I	Angel T-Shirt-Printed ___ S ___ M ___ L ___XL		_____ x 15.00 =	_____
	Qty Qty Qty Qty			
J	Angel Tank Top-Printed ___ S ___ M ___ L ___ XL		_____ x 15.00 =	_____
	Qty Qty Qty Qty			
K	Angel Mugs		_____ x 12.00 =	_____
L	Angel of the Sea Miniature (3" x 3" x 3")		_____ x 15.00 =	_____
M	Cape May Light House Miniature (3" x 3" x 4" High)		_____ x 15.00 =	_____

Sub Total = _____

Shipping & Handling 3.00 per item = _____

NJ Residents Add 6% Sales Tax = _____

Total = _____

Name: _____

Address: _____

_____ Phone: _____ - _____ - _____

Credit Card: ____ Visa ____ Master Card   Exp. date: _____

Card#: _____   Signature: _____

Prices Subject to Change Without Notice

The Angel of Cape May, Inc.
34 Tuckahoe Rd. #361
Marmora, NJ 08223-1206